John W. Schaum
Music History Speller

Preface

This unique writing book consists of a series of music history stories. Many of the words appear in notation so that the student will need to read the notes in order to comprehend each composer's biography.

The *Music History Speller* is recommended for all music students. This music speller may be used for instrumental students, piano students, or for general classroom use. The contents are especially valuable for study in music appreciation classes. Music appreciation and note-reading are developed simultaneously.

The stories may be used in three ways:

1. As a reader: The student may simply read the stories.
2. As a note speller: The student writes out the letter names.
3. As a performance book: The student plays the notes on the piano.

D1385291

John W. Schaum
Music History Speller

CONTENTS

Johann Sebastian Bach
1685 - 1750

At the [♪] of ten, Bach [♪] -me an orphan. His

brother then [♪] -n to take [♪] -re of him. Brother Christoph would

also t- [♪] -h Johann music. Once young [♪] -h pro- [♪]

to copy some of his brother's music. Christoph [♪] -me m- [♪] and

called it [♪] and took it away. Johann [♪]

to have it [♪] -k [♪] -use he h- [♪] worked like

[♪] -ver. But his brother was [♪] to his pl- [♪]

Nevertheless Johann's [♪] - orts didn't [♪] and he

su- [♪] in [♪] -oming [♪] -mous. He once won

a [♪] [♪] -use of his good organ playing.

The [♪] -s of Bach [♪] to the progress of music.

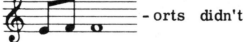

George Frideric Handel
1685 - 1759

Handel's  for-  him to

musician, but told him to pro-  to  -ome a lawyer. Handel

dr-  this and slyly 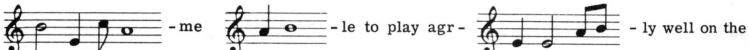 -n to practice in the attic and soon

 -me  -le to play agr-  -ly well on the

clavichord, which is a gr-  -t  -l like our piano. One  -y

he r- 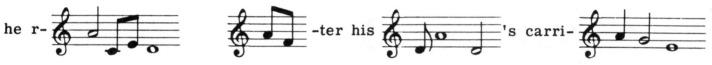 -ter his 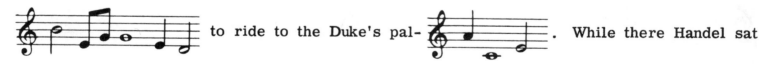 's carri-  and

to ride to the Duke's pal-  . While there Handel sat

on the  of the organ  -nch and pro-

to play. The Duke's   -med happily and he

pl-  with the  to let Handel

musician. Fr-  from legal study, he later wrote "The Messiah".

1714 - 1787

When Gluck was a 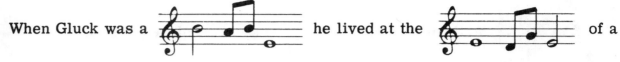 he lived at the  of a

forest in Germany. He loved to 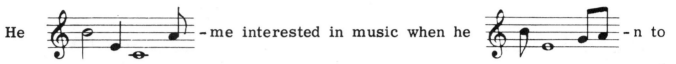 the birds and watch the  -s

at work. He  -me interested in music when he  -n to

 pupil at the  -my of Prague. Here, he

pro- 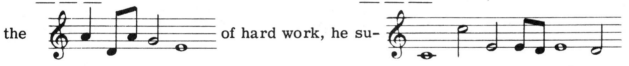 to  -rn his living by singing and playing. Later he

 -ided to go to Italy to 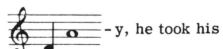 -ome an opera student. By following

the  of hard work, he su- 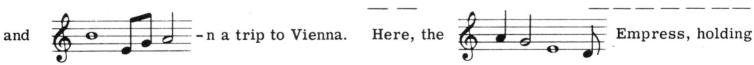 in writing and

producing seven operas. He also studied counterpoint which is the art of  -ing

one or more tunes to another tune. One  -y, he took his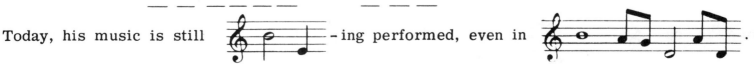

and [note] -n a trip to Vienna. Here, the [note] Empress, holding

her gorgeous [note] [note] , listened to one of Gluck's operas.

Today, his music is still [note] -ing performed, even in [note] .

EL01030A

Franz Joseph Haydn
1732 - 1809

At home, Haydn's  played the harp by -r, his

mother sang, and young Joseph  away on the drum. When still a

l- , only six years of  his parents agr- to let Joseph

leave home to study music. He wasn't always  enough, but he learned a great

 -l. Soon he  -me a choir boy. Joseph thought

that  , (another choir boy) was  . So he went

ah-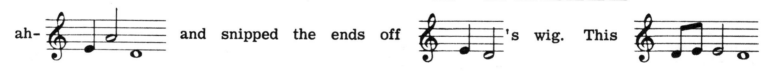 and snipped the ends off  's wig. This

 -used young Haydn to 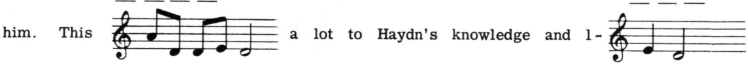 expelled. Later the great musician

Porpora,  -me interested in Haydn and offered to t- -h

him. This  a lot to Haydn's knowledge and l-

him to su- in  -veloping the symphony.

Wolfgang Amadeus Mozart

1756 - 1791

At an [note] when most children are learning their [note]'s

Wolfgang Mozart was r- [note] -ing notes and making up his own tunes. His

[note] was [note] musician and [note] -n to give Wolfgang harpsichord

lessons at the [note] of four. The l- [note] 's [note] was full of

fun and he enjoyed playing [note] -s on his friends. His musical [note] -s

were so extraordinary that his [note] took him on trips to play concerts. They took

their [note] in a carriage [note] -use they didn't have

[note] -s then. In the evening when the sun [note] away, they would stop

at a [note] to eat. No doubt, Wolfgang loved [note] -burgers for

his [note] . After the journey, he would [note] all tired

out and ready for [note] . In later life, he didn't get enough [note] -s from

his music to live comfortably, but his music will never [note] .

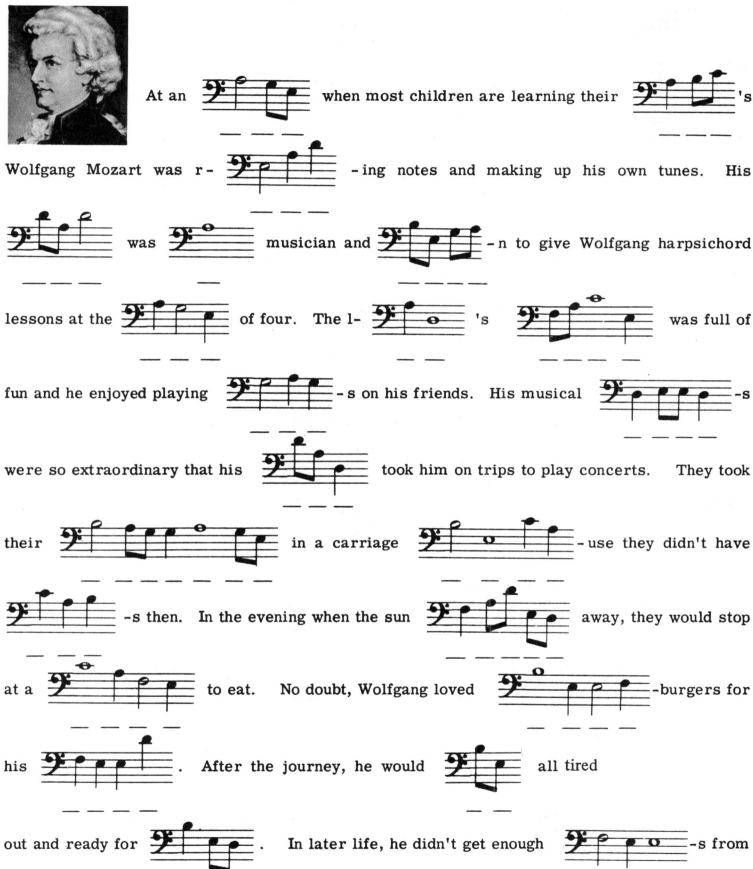

Ludwig van Beethoven
1770 - 1827

It was in the 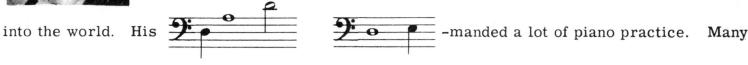 of Napoleon that Beethoven  -me

into the world. His 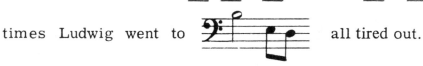  -manded a lot of piano practice. Many

times Ludwig went to 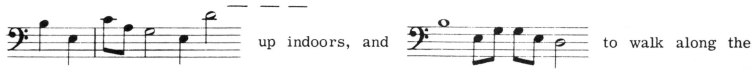 all tired out. He didn't like to

 up indoors, and 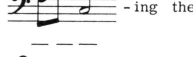 to walk along the

 of the forest  -ing the wind. In spite of his strict

 , Ludwig su- 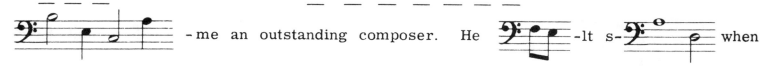 in liking music and

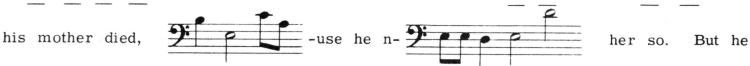 -me an outstanding composer. He  -lt s-  when

his mother died,  -use he n- 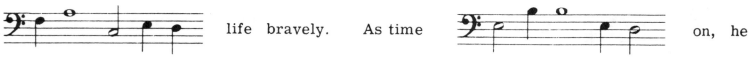 her so. But he

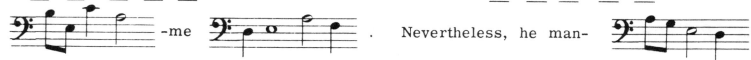 life bravely. As time  on, he

 -me 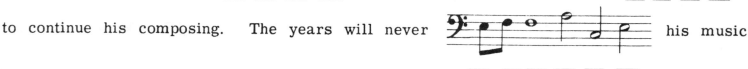 . Nevertheless, he man-

to continue his composing. The years will never 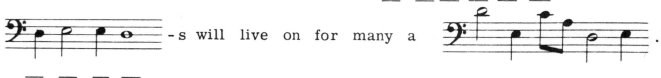 his music

and his  -s will live on for many a .

EL01030A

1797 - 1828

Franz Schubert h-  musical  -r at an

 -rly  . Like most children he was 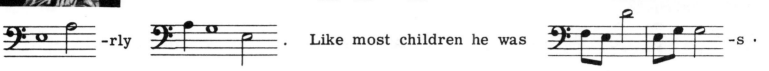 -s .

for breakfast. He 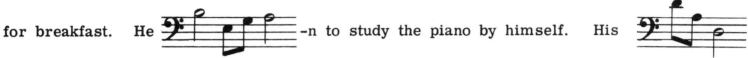 -n to study the piano by himself. His

was a schoolmaster so when Franz n- 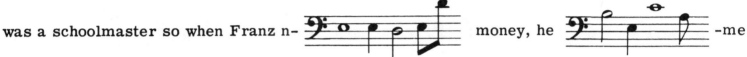 money, he 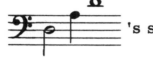 -me

a t- 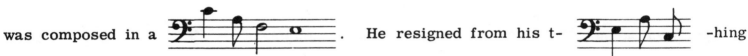 -her in his 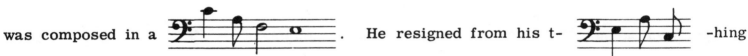 's school. His song "Hark! Hark! the Lark"

was composed in a  . He resigned from his t-  -hing

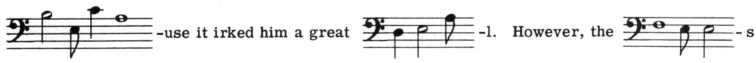 -use it irked him a great  -l. However, the  -s

from his compositions  little to his n-  -s. His

pocket book would often 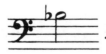 . He will always 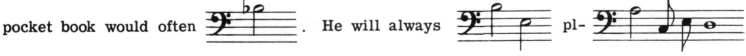 pl-

as a 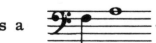 -mous song writer. Neither  nor an

 will ever  the  -me of Schubert.

EL01030A

Gioacchino Rossini
1792 - 1868

Rossini su-  during his lifetime in

 -oming the r- 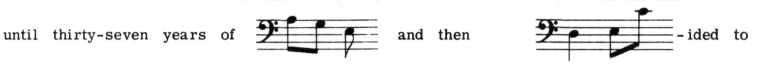 of the music world. He h-

more money than he n-  . He worked st- 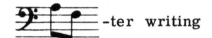 -ily

until thirty-seven years of 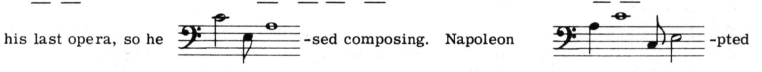 and then  -ided to

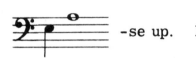 -se up. He  -me nervous 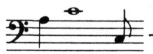 -ter writing

his last opera, so he 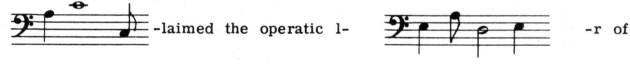 -sed composing. Napoleon 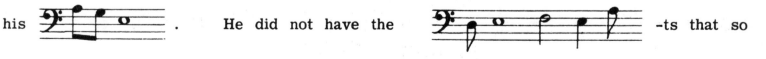 -pted

Rossini's music with gr- 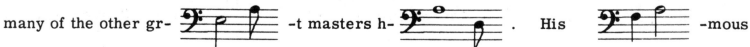 -t 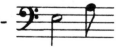 -tion. Everywhere

Rossini was  -laimed the operatic l-  -r of

his  . He did not have the  -ts that so

many of the other gr- -t masters h- . His -mous

"William Tell Overture" is in- on the all time hit par-

-ch -y Mrs. Mendelssohn would play and sing for her -r -mily of four children. Their -s -med with -light. -lix was to -ome the musician of the -mily and to the glory of the -less art of music. -lix h- a sister named -nny who was also musical. She -rly loved to wear a dress with blue, with which she -rried a white su- -ing in -oming a - mous composer himself, Mendelssohn did a great -l to make a pl- for -h's music in the world.

EL01030A

Frédéric Chopin
1810 - 1849

Frederic [♪] -n lessons at the [♪] of six and [♪] -ore he was twelve, he wrote a march. His [♪] en- [♪] the musician Elsner to t- [♪] -h Frederic composition. At seventeen, Chopin [♪] -rly [♪] -voted himself entirely to music. His skillful piano playing [♪] -led the audience. [♪] -ter a time, he [♪] -me ill and dr- [♪] the i- [♪] of [♪] -ing [♪] up in the city, so he took his [♪] and went to the p- [♪] -ul island of Majorca. But this didn't help, [♪] -use his strength [♪] away. So he took [♪] and [♪] [♪] -k to the city. The [♪] of his [♪] -ys he spent in Paris. He proved to [♪] the greatest piano composer of his [♪] or any other [♪].

EL01030A

Robert Schumann
1810 - 1856

Schumann [♪] -n music study at first in a [♪] -sual way, but soon [♪] -ided to [♪] -vote his life to it. His mother [♪] him not to [♪] -ome a musician but to [♪] lawyer inst- [♪] . However, his mother [♪] -n to notice that most of the time, he would en- [♪] in piano playing or in r- [♪] -ing p- [♪] [♪] -ter p- [♪] of mystery stories. She finally allowed him to B♮ and [♪] -ome a pupil of the great t- [♪] -her, Frederick Wieck, whose [♪] -ughter, Clara, later [♪] -me Robert's wife. Schumann invented a [♪] -vice to strengthen his fourth finger. This proved to [♪] [♪] In [♪] -t it ruined his hand and m- [♪] it impossible to go ah- [♪] with his playing [♪] -reer. May- [♪] this was an [♪] -t of [♪] -te, [♪] -use it l- [♪] him to [♪] -ome a composer.

EL01030A

Franz Liszt
1811 - 1886

The first name of Franz Liszt's  was  -m.

Franz 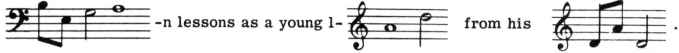 -n lessons as a young l-  from his  .

He  -ve a concert at the 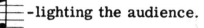 of nine which su-

in 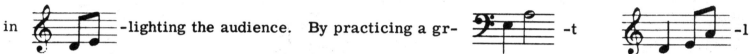 -lighting the audience. By practicing a gr-  -t  -l

he 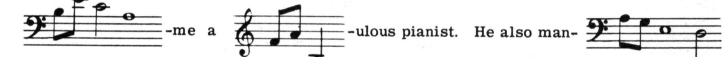 -me a  -ulous pianist. He also man-

to  -ome 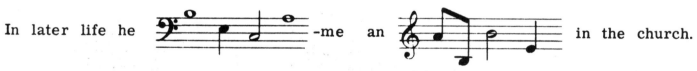 -mous both by his composing and arranging.

In later life he  -me an in the church. He

practi-  -verishly, 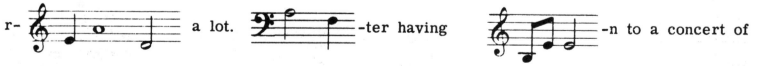 -ve lessons, and

r-  a lot.  -ter having  -n to a concert of

W- -ner's music, Liszt -ught a cold which -used

his  -th. He was perhaps the greatest pianist of all time.

Richard Wagner
1813 - 1883

Soon ⎢ -ter Richard Wagner h- ⎢ -n born he lost his ⎢ . Later, his mother ⎢ -me en- ⎢ and married Ludwig Geyer who predicted that some ⎢ -y Richard would ⎢ -ome ⎢ -mous. The l- ⎢ -n piano lessons at the ⎢ of eleven. His t- ⎢ -her wasn't too pleased ⎢ -use Richard didn't h- ⎢ the rules but inst- ⎢ played by ⎢ -r, tunes that would pop into his h- ⎢ . He also ⎢ -n to r- ⎢ the opera scores of Mozart, and pro- ⎢ to ⎢ to his knowl- ⎢ . Wagner's greatest ⎢ -s were in opera. At first, people paid no h- ⎢ to him but later they ⎢ -pted him. His ⎢ -me will endure for many ⎢ .

Giuseppi Verdi
1813 - 1901

One 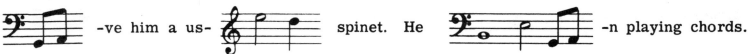-y when Verdi was a l-, his -ve him a us- spinet. He -n playing chords.

One pleased him a great -l. But when he tried to bring it -k to life, he couldn't find it. This -t -led him, and he flew into a r-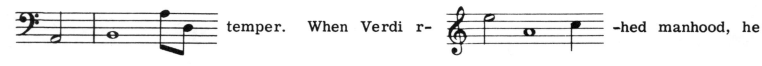. He almost 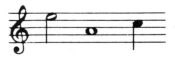 the spinet.

His 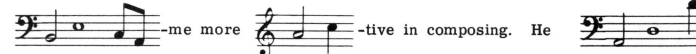 -me in the nick of time, and -ve the l-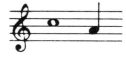 some good -vice -out not having  temper. When Verdi r--hed manhood, he -me more -tive in composing. He many operas to the list of great music. Verdi h- his share of s- and gl- moments. At the of eighty-eight, he passed away.

EL01030A

1825 - 1899

When the 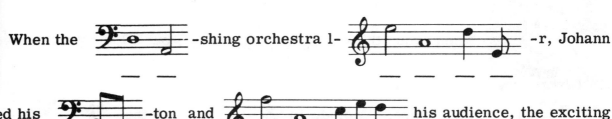 -shing orchestra l- 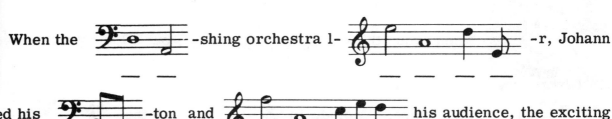 -r, Johann

Strauss, Jr., lifted his  -ton and  his audience, the exciting

 -ts of the waltz  -ve everyone a rhythmic tr-  -t.

There was a gr- 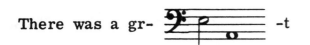 -t 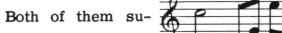 -l of jealousy  -tween young

Strauss and his  . Both of them su-  in

 -ining  -me as waltz writers. However, Johann, Jr.

 -me the "Waltz King" 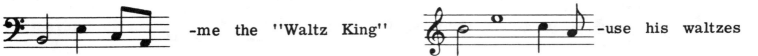 -use his waltzes

h-  the list on the hit par- 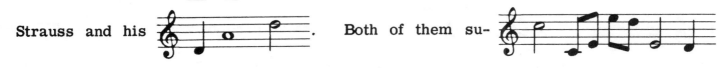 of that 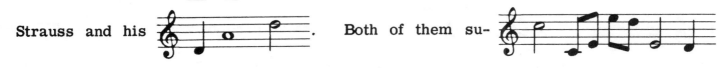 -y.

Young Strauss 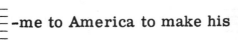 -me to America to make his 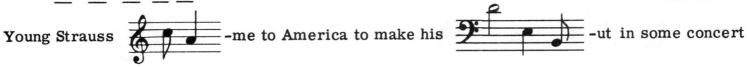 -ut in some concert

en- 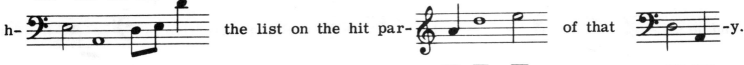 -ments. He was 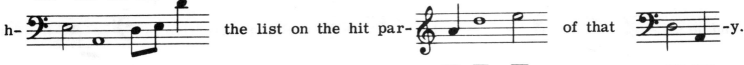 -pted with st- 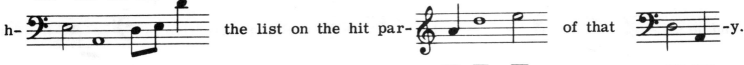 -y

enthusiasm. But Vienna was the  -rest pl-  on  -rth

for him and he went 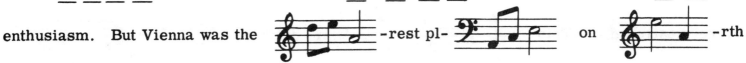 -k to spend the 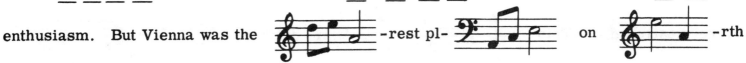 of his 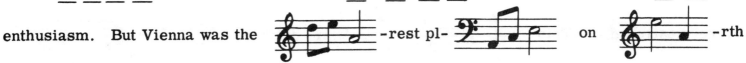 -ys there.

Anton Rubinstein
1829 - 1894

When you think 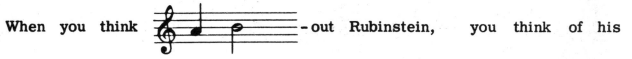 -out Rubinstein, you think of his

-mous piece, "Melody in 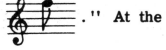 ." At the of five, he took

lessons from the  -st piano t- -her in Moscow. His mother

h- him tutored inst- 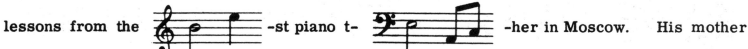 of sending him to school. Thus,

the l-  -me a child prodigy and -ve

concerts. In 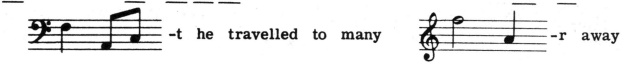 -t he travelled to many -r away

pl-  -s giving recitals. Composing  -n to interest him

and he pro- to  -velop his creative i-  -s.

Some  luck  -me on one of his trips. -use

of passport difficulty, all the manuscripts in his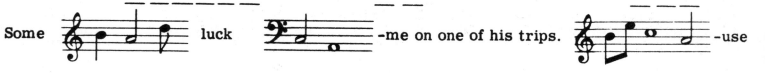

were destroyed. This  -ir didn't 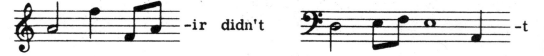 -t

him. He went ah- and m- a fresh start.

Brahms' 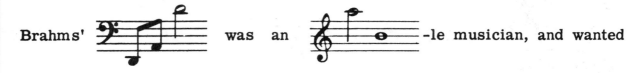 was an 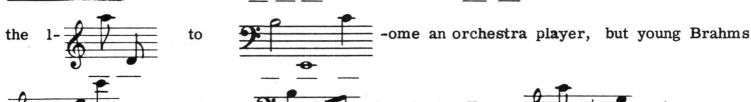 -le musician, and wanted

the l-  to  -ome an orchestra player, but young Brahms

 -ided to  -in piano. He m- 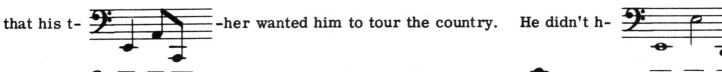 such progress

that his t-  -her wanted him to tour the country. He didn't h-

this  -vice but inst- 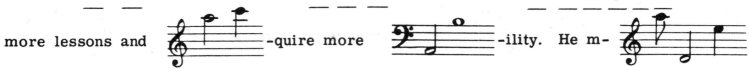 , pro-  to take

more lessons and 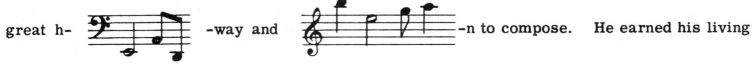 -quire more  -ility. He m-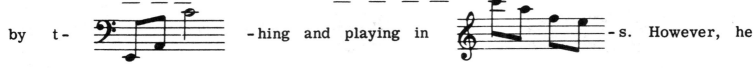

great h-  -way and 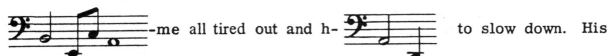 -n to compose. He earned his living

by t- 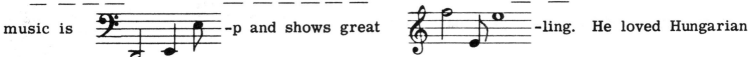 -hing and playing in -s. However, he

 -me all tired out and h- to slow down. His

music is -p and shows great -ling. He loved Hungarian

tunes  -rly and used them in his work. Brahms 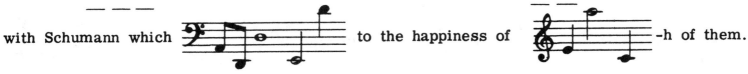 -veloped a friendship

with Schumann which to the happiness of -h of them.

Georges Bizet
1838 - 1875

Bizet's ♪ was a singing t- ♪ -her. This -kground helped him to ♪ -ome a successful opera composer. He lived p- ♪ -ully in Paris, t- ♪ -hing, playing the piano and composing. He ♪ -me en- ♪ to his t- ♪ -her's daughter and married her. They m- ♪ an agr- ♪ -le couple. Bizet n- ♪ encour- ♪ -ment ♪ -ly. He was s- ♪ ♪ -use he didn't su- ♪ right away. His opera ♪ -rmen was not ♪ -pted with great success until a ♪ -w months ♪ -ore his ♪ -th. ♪ -ter that, it h- ♪ a st- ♪ -y rise in popularity. To - ♪ -y it is still one of the ♪ -st operas on the st- ♪ . ♪ sure to s- ♪ it if you ♪ -n.

Peter Ilych Tschaikowsky
1840 - 1893

As a l-  of four, Peter 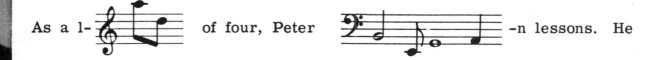 -n lessons. He

m-  rapid h-  -way and soon  -n to

compose. At fourteen he was s-  -ned by his mother's sudden

-th. Without the  -tion of his mother, he

-me very lonely. It hurt Tschaikowsky  -ply and in much

of his music there is a  -ling of s- 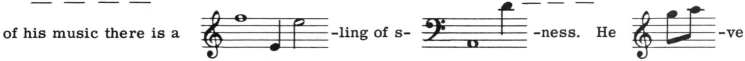 -ness. He  -ve

lessons during the  -y to  -rn his living. Later in li- 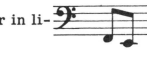,

a wealthy widow fr-  him from money worries so he 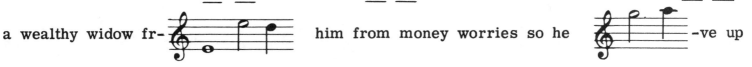 -ve up

t-  -hing and pro- 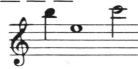 to give all his time to composing.

This m-  it possible for him to  -ome one of the world's

great composers. His 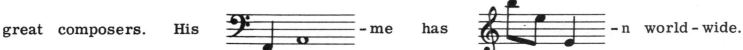 -me has -n world-wide.

EL01030A

Anton Dvořák
1841 - 1904

Dvorak h-  who owned a small

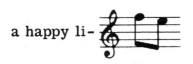 in a vill-  in Bohemia. As a l-  he l-

a happy li-  . At fifteen, he  his  to let him

enter the music  -my at Prague. He could  -rely

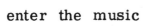 -ord to go, but he went ah- 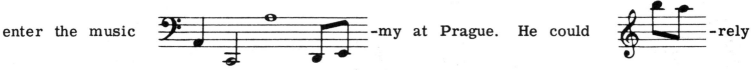 and  -rned his

own way. He was 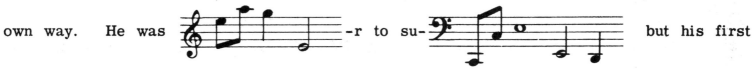 -r to su- but his first

 -orts did not click. In 1878, his Slavonic  -nces brought him

 -me. Later he  -me 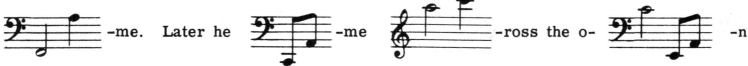 -ross the o-  -n

to America and  -me interested in the  -uty of negro folk

tunes. These he m-  use of in his "New World Symphony." The i-

that America h- its own folk music was first m- known by Dvorak.

Edvard Grieg
1843 - 1907

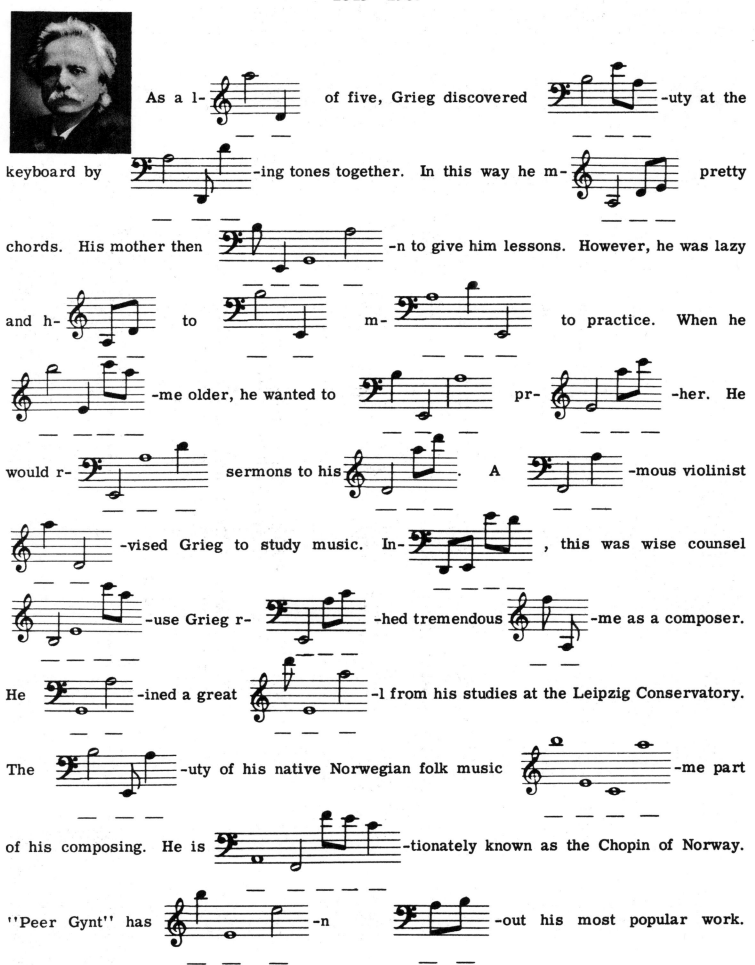

As a l- [♪] of five, Grieg discovered [♪] -uty at the keyboard by [♪] -ing tones together. In this way he m- [♪] pretty chords. His mother then [♪] -n to give him lessons. However, he was lazy and h- [♪] to [♪] m- [♪] to practice. When he [♪] -me older, he wanted to [♪] pr- [♪] -her. He would r- [♪] sermons to his [♪]. A [♪] -mous violinist [♪] -vised Grieg to study music. In- [♪] , this was wise counsel [♪] -use Grieg r- [♪] -hed tremendous [♪] -me as a composer. He [♪] -ined a great [♪] -l from his studies at the Leipzig Conservatory. The [♪] -uty of his native Norwegian folk music [♪] -me part of his composing. He is [♪] -tionately known as the Chopin of Norway. "Peer Gynt" has [♪] -n [♪] -out his most popular work.

EL01030A

Claude Debussy
1862 - 1918

-ussy liked to -lled Clau- . His aunt -me his tutor when he was a l- . In -t, she was his only t- -her in r- -ing and writing. He saw -uty in small objects. This -ted his later pieces in which he tr- -ted music in a subdued manner. He to his honors by winning for first pl- in composing. -h year, he -me more -mous. -ussy's music consists mainly of harmony inst- of melody. Where the older composers h- -n writing things ever bi- -r and louder, Debussy pro- to r- -h great musical -ling in a small quiet way.

Sergei Rachmaninoff
1873 - 1943

One of Rachmaninoff's  -rly compositions won a gold

 at the music  -my in Moscow. Later,

the Revolution m - 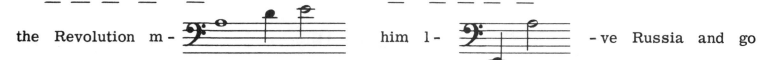 him l-  -ve Russia and go

ah -  with his  -reer in America. Here, Rachmaninoff

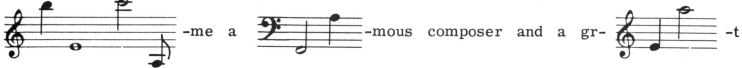 -me a  -mous composer and a gr- 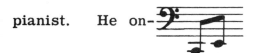 -t

pianist. He on- 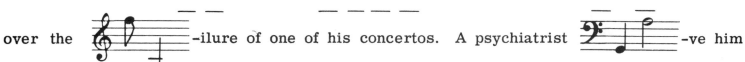 -me  -pressed

over the  -ilure of one of his concertos. A psychiatrist  -ve him

some help and  -in he went  -k to his composing with

new  -rness. He m-  many concert tours and wrote

a st-  -y str-  -m of pieces. His music  -ls

with -p -ling and appeals to every .

EL01030A

Stephen Foster
1826 - 1864

Stephen Foster was born in a small vill-  in Pennsylvania.

When only of two he m-  music on a guitar. As

a l-  , his 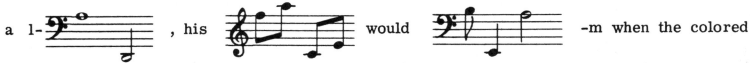 would  -m when the colored

people sang. His folks -vised him not to en- 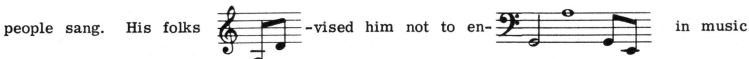 in music

as a  -reer. But he m-  up his mind to

composer and  -me America's greatest folk-song writer. He

-ve -out two-hundred songs to the world. But the world

-ve him very little in  -s. He did not su-

financially. Inst-  he chose to su-  musically. The

-uty of his songs are  -r to the h-  -rts of everyone.

1862 - 1901

Even at an  -rly  , Nevin was  -r

to l- 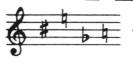 -rn 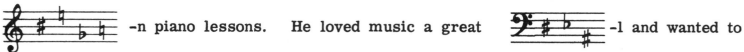 -out music. As a l-  of eight he

 -n piano lessons. He loved music a great  -l and wanted to

  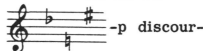 musician. However, his 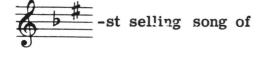 -vised a business

-reer. -ter -p discour- -ment, Nevin was

  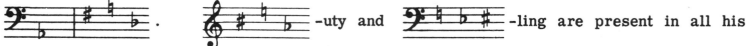

finally allowed to go ah-  with his music. The -st selling song of

all -s is the "Rosary" by Nevin. His piano piece "Narcissus"  -me

-uty and -ling are present in all his

music. He never m-  enough money to  -re very well financially.

His music r- -hed greatest -me -ter his

-th. Nevin cannot  classed as a great composer but he

 -n -pted as a sincere writer of light music.

Edward MacDowell
1861 - 1908

Mac Dowell when he was a l- 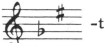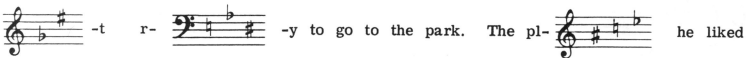 , loved to help the  -mily

-t r- 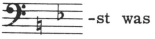 -y to go to the park. The pl-  he liked

-st was 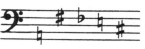 -ntral Park. Although he h-  -n

born in New York City, his  -tion was in the 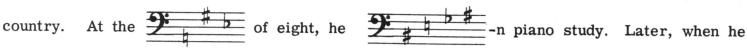 -uty of the

country. At the  of eight, he  -n piano study. Later, when he

r- -hed manhood and  -me a composer, his pieces

-picted his  -p  -ling for nature. At the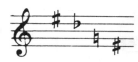

of the woods, he would look up and s-  an  -le in flight. He loved

the 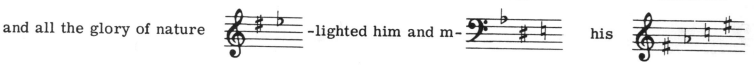 -h and the s- . The  -r and the -s

and all the glory of nature -lighted him and m- his

-m. America  -n proud of Edward MacDowell.

EL01030A

Victor Herbert's 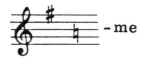 -me 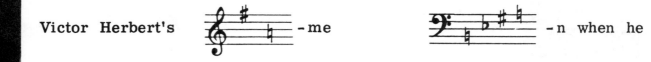 -n when he

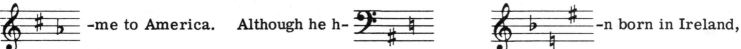 -me to America.   Although he h- 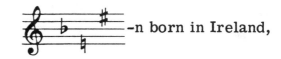 -n born in Ireland,

his musical 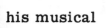 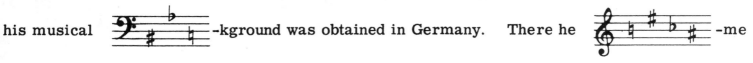 -kground was obtained in Germany.   There he  -me

en- 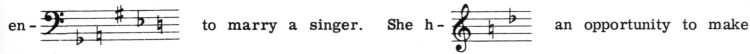 to marry a singer.   She h-  an opportunity to make

her singing 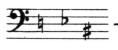 -ut in America.   She wouldn't  -pt it unless

Victor -me along.   He couldn't 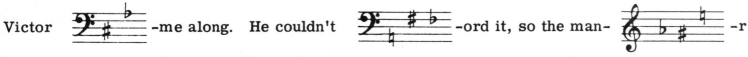 -ord it, so the man-  -r

m-  a  -l whereby Victor could -rn his way by

playing 'cello.  -ter playing for many st- 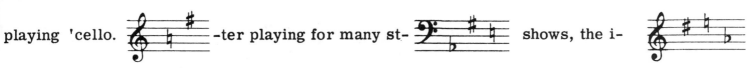 shows, the i-

entered his h-  to try composing.   He su- 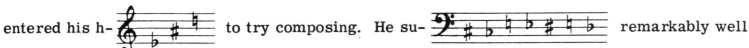 remarkably well

and man- to -ome one of America's outstanding composers.

EL01030A

John Philip Sousa

1854 - 1932

As a l-  , Sousa was 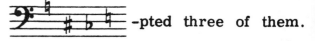 -r to learn music.

He won five music 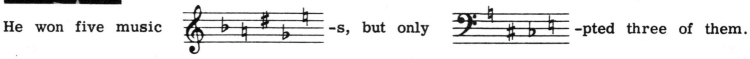 -s, but only 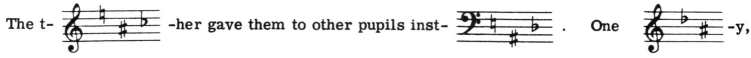 -pted three of them.

The t-   -her gave them to other pupils inst-  . One 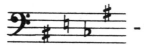 -y,

Sousa's t-  -her h-  a severe h- -he

and flew into a r- 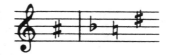 -use John Philip m-

a mistake. This h- 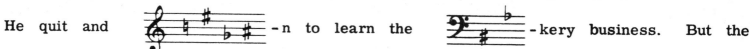 -t on Sousa.

He quit and  -n to learn the  -kery business. But the

long hours m- him all tired out so he went -k

to his t-  -her and they -me good friends once more.

Sousa's 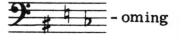 -vised his son to join the Marines as a

 -nd and music apprentice. This l- to his -oming

a 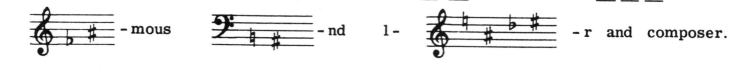 -mous -nd l- -r and composer.

Composer Recognition Quiz

DIRECTIONS: Below is a numbered list of all the composers presented in this book. The pictures of these musicians are also reproduced but in a different order. On the dotted line underneath each picture you are to identify each composer by writing the number of his name. Thus, the first picture is Rossini so the number eight has been written underneath. The correct answers are printed upside down at the bottom of this page.

1. Bach	8. Rossini	15. Strauss	22. Debussy
2. Handel	9. Mendelssohn	16. Rubinstein	23. Rachmaninoff
3. Gluck	10. Chopin	17. Brahms	24. Foster
4. Haydn	11. Schumann	18. Bizet	25. Nevin
5. Mozart	12. Liszt	19. Tschaikowsky	26. Mac Dowell
6. Beethoven	13. Wagner	20. Dvorak	27. Herbert
7. Schubert	14. Verdi	21. Grieg	28. Sousa

...8...   ....

....

....

....

EL01030A

SCHAUM SOLO PIANO ALBUMS FOR THE YOUNG STUDENT

An enjoyable series for recreational playing

These Schaum books offer the perfect solution for student motivation—appealing collections of orginal works and all–time favorite arrangements. Each book is 24 pages in length. The John W. Schaum SOLO PIANO ALBUMS correlate with most piano courses, and they will please students of all ages.

Levels 1 and 2

The Boogie Book
__ (EL00869A)

The Broadway Book
__ (EL03489)

The Christmas Book
__ (EL03212)

The Country Book
__ (EL03503)

The Folk Song Book
__ (EL00871A)

The Gay Nineties Book
__ (EL00872)

The Girls Book
__ (EL01027)

The Movie Book
__ (EL03284)

The Parade Book
__ (EL00874)

The Ragtime Book
__ (EL01029A)

The Recital Book
__ (EL00876)

The Sacred Book
__ (EL00877)

The TV Book
__ (EL03573)

The Waltz Book
__ (EL00878)

The 70s Book
__ (EL03718)

The 80s Book
__ (EL03669)

This music is available from your favorite music dealer.

AD 0314A